Original title:
Under the Tropical Sky

Copyright © 2025 Creative Arts Management OÜ
All rights reserved.

Author: Franklin Stone
ISBN HARDBACK: 978-1-80581-530-3
ISBN PAPERBACK: 978-1-80581-057-5
ISBN EBOOK: 978-1-80581-530-3

Echoes of Laughter on the Coast

Seagulls squawk in silly glee,
As beach balls bounce like they're set free.
Sandy toes and crazy hats,
Chasing waves while we're all like cats.

Ice cream drips down cone's side,
Melting fast, oh what a ride!
Laughter mixes with the tide,
In this fun-filled, sunny stride.

Tides of Time Beneath Swaying Palms

Palm trees dance, a comic show,
Their leafy fronds, a silly glow.
Crabs do a crabby little jig,
While flip-flops flung like a wild pig.

Time escapes with each warm breeze,
Tickling our toes, just like it sees.
Shells sing songs of silly pride,
As we trip and laugh down the tide.

A Journey Through Eden's Breath

Bright flowers giggle, colors pop,
Bumblebees buzzing, can't stop, won't stop.
Banana peels make quite the slip,
Oh, what fun on this laughter trip!

Coconuts roll with a clumsy thud,
Falling down from trees with a thud!
Laughter echoes through the air,
Creating joy beyond compare.

Fireflies Glittering in the Twilight

Fireflies flicker like stars at play,
They dance in circles, in their own ballet.
Grasshoppers join with a jump and hop,
As we giggle together, never stop.

The night wraps us in a happy shroud,
Silly faces, bright joys, we're loud.
With every flicker comes a cheer,
Under the glow, fun is here!

Lush Hills Cradling Celestial Dreams

In the hills where chickens roam,
A goat wears sunglasses like a gnome.
Palm trees dance with silly glee,
While parrots gossip—did you see?

The monkeys plot a heist of fruit,
Dressed in capes, they're quite the hoot.
A fruit pie fight breaks out in sight,
As laughter echoes into the night.

The Color of Sunsets and Sighs

Bees buzz 'round in neon hats,
While crabs take part in silly chats.
We wave at clouds that wink and tease,
As ice cream melts upon the breeze.

The sun drips gold on laughing waves,
While seagulls dive as if they crave.
With every splash, a giggle spills,
As time stands still, joy-filled thrills.

Journeys Woven in Coconut Fronds

A coconut rolls down the lane,
Chasing a kid who's lost his brain.
Flip-flops flapping, laughter flies,
As pirates search for hidden fries.

Kites dangle low, caught in a tree,
"Look, mom, I'm flying!" shouts a bee.
Each frond a stage for antics grand,
As nature's clowns take their stand.

A Flavor of Mango Days

Mango juice spills on sandy toes,
While beach balls bounce, and laughter flows.
Sandy poodles strut with flair,
In sunglasses bold, they're quite a pair.

Kids on surfboards chase the tide,
With jellyfish and a friendly glide.
A splash, a joke, a silly dance,
As life unfolds, we take a chance.

Starlit Tales by the Lagoon

Beneath the sparkly dome so high,
Fishes wear hats as they swim by.
Crabs dance on sand in a funny jig,
While turtles play chess, each thinks he's big.

The moon gives a wink to the clowns in shells,
Octopus tells jokes, everyone yells!
A parrot squawks out a wild old tune,
As laughter echoes, all under the moon.

Embrace of the Warm Ocean

The sun's a big ball of melted cheese,
And waves are just whispers from the breeze.
Seagulls roller skate on liquid gold,
While dolphins plot pranks, oh so bold.

A fish in a bow tie swims with flair,
Throwing a party, it's quite the affair.
Mermaids sip cocktails, flip their hair,
Sharing wild stories without any care.

Nature's Canvas in Vibrant Hues

Colors splash like jelly on toast,
Bees wear sunglasses, a funky host.
Flowers giggle, their petals all swirl,
While butterflies dance in a dizzy twirl.

The sky's a painter with a big brush,
Clouds play hide and seek, creating a hush.
Lemurs wear coats, thinking they're cool,
While chameleons joke, 'This hue is a rule!'

Rhythm of Waves at Dusk

The waves tap beats like an old drum,
While crabs grab spoons, ready for fun.
Stars start to twinkle, the beach is a stage,
Where jellyfish boogie, jumping with rage!

The seaweed swings in a gentle flow,
As clams gossip secrets, all in a row.
A lighthouse dances, shining so bright,
In this wild soirée by the ocean's light.

Beneath the Lush Canopy

Silly monkeys swing with glee,
Wearing hats from our last spree.
Parrots squawk with endless flair,
Flapping wings, they break the air.

Bright coconuts hang in a row,
I reached up high, but fell below.
Laughter echoes through the trees,
As I land beneath the leaves.

Whispers of the Warm Breeze

The breeze carries my hat away,
Chasing it down, I start to sway.
A squirrel giggles, what a tease,
As I trip over roots with ease.

Fruits fall down like nature's rain,
Squished bananas are my gain.
I slip and slide, it's quite a show,
The jungle floor becomes my stage, oh no!

Dance of the Sunlit Palms

The palm trees sway, they start to dance,
I join in for a silly prance.
Fronds like skirts that tickle the breeze,
I spin round, with joy I seize.

A crab calls out from the sand,
"Keep it down, it's getting grand!"
I twirl again, without a care,
"Just let me dance, I swear, I swear!"

Secrets of the Evening Rain

The raindrops fall, they tickle my toes,
With every splash, my laughter grows.
Rainbow puddles form a stage,
For frogs and I to act our age.

The night sings songs of silly dreams,
While fireflies join in with gleams.
I tap-dance in mud, oh what a sight,
Even the stars are laughing tonight!

Secrets in the Canopy Above

Parrots squawk in a clumsy dance,
Monkeys giggle at their chance.
Leaves are whispers of cheeky tales,
As squirrels plot their nutty trails.

Sunlight spills through a leafy hat,
While shadows giggle, imagine that!
A lizard starts a game of tag,
While sleepy sloths just sit and brag.

A Mosaic of Nature's Palette

Colors drip from the painter's brush,
As crickets chirp in a curious hush.
The flowers wink, a flirtatious tease,
While frogs croak jokes that aim to please.

Butterflies wear the brightest hues,
While bumblebees buzz with unwarranted news.
Each creature, an artist, bold and spry,
In this gallery of laughter, oh my, oh my!

Tidepools of Memories and Dreams

Starfish lounge in their rocky bed,
While sea cucumbers plot ahead.
A crab tells tales with quite a flair,
Of pirates' ghosts and mermaid hair.

Seashells giggle, tossed by the tide,
As minnows dart in a playful glide.
A seaweed band starts up a tune,
While jellyfish dance by the light of the moon.

Tropical Breezes and Kindred Spirits

Palm trees sway to a breezy beat,
While toucans strut with such a feat.
Coconuts throw parties in the sand,
With crabs on the mic, oh isn't it grand?

The sun smiles down, a friendly chap,
As flip-flops race in a goofy lap.
Laughter bubbles like soda pop,
In this paradise, we never stop.

Tranquility Beneath Whispering Palms

The coconuts wobble, oh what a sight,
A monkey stole one, he took off in flight.
With a sip of sweet juice, I start to sway,
While the breeze laughs by, taking my hat away.

Sunsets paint gold on the ocean's face,
Flip-flops get tangled, oh what a chase!
A crab skitters past, quite sure of his path,
While I trip and stumble, it's all just a laugh.

The hammock's swaying, my drink's gone too,
Did it float away or slip from my view?
With giggles surrounding, the stars twinkle bright,
These silly moments are pure delight.

So if you should ponder, where's the real bliss?
It's here amidst chaos, you'll find it like this.
Between laughter and snacks, there's joy to reclaim,
In this wacky paradise, we've all gone a bit insane.

Sunbeams Entwined with Laughter

Sunbeams are dancing on my bright nose,
While a lizard stares, judging my clothes.
In shades of pastel, we're striking a pose,
But the sunscreen's gone rogue, now my leg's like a rose.

Drinks overflow with umbrellas so grand,
A parrot swoops down, it's a party on land!
With a squawk and a flap, it steals my last fry,
Guess it's birdie brunch; oh, why oh why?

The beach ball is wobbling, it's about to burst,
Don't blame the kids, but hey, I feel cursed!
With giggles and splashes, we make quite a scene,
A wild ocean circus, we're all so obscene!

Golden sunsets splash memories galore,
Don't mind the sand stuck right to my core.
As laughter erupts, we're lost in the tide,
In sunbeam-filled moments, our worries all slide.

The Essence of Jasmine in the Night

The jasmine blooms wildly, a fragrant delight,
Yet I'm sneezing and wheezing, oh what a fright!
With fireflies flickering, they dance in the dark,
While I swat like a ninja, what's that in my park?

A barbecue's smoking, the burgers may burn,
While I strike up the band, it's my time to turn.
With spatula in hand, I'm the king of the grill,
But the sausages fumble; oh, what a thrill!

The moon's shining brightly, it's the perfect scene,
But the neighbors are blasting some beats quite obscene.
We're all laughing so hard, it's a real summer dream,
As we dance in the backyard, or so it would seem!

So let's toast with a soda, raise your cup high,
To sneezes and giggles beneath the dark sky.
With the essence of jasmine that lingers tonight,
We'll cherish the fun till we say our goodnight.

Kisses from a Warm Breeze

A warm breeze tickles, how it loves to tease,
It swoops through my hair, like it's trying to please.
With a sunhat that's flying, we both lose control,
As I chase down the hat, giggling all on a roll.

The ocean waves crash, bringing laughter near,
Each splash seems to echo our joy and our cheer.
With sandy toes wriggling, and laughter that grows,
Who knew beach days would come with such woes?

A seagull swoops down, searching for fries,
And I shout, "Hey buddy, that's not a surprise!"
Yet I'm laughing so hard, it's unclear who won,
In this wacky wind dance, we're all just having fun.

So come join the madness, where giggles run free,
Life's far too short, let's all just agree.
With kisses from breezes and sunshine so bright,
Let's treasure these moments, our hearts feel just right.

Stars Over Sapphire Waves

Stars giggle like children in flight,
As waves chuckle, splashing the night.
A crab in a tuxedo dances with flair,
While fish wear sunglasses, without a care.

Jellyfish waltz in a translucent dress,
While seagulls debate who's the best at the mess.
A dolphin flips pancakes, quite the surprise,
Under the twinkle of shimmering skies.

The moon tries a dive, but just makes a splash,
As night-blooming flowers join in with a bash.
Laughter bubbles up from the deepest green,
Nature's comedy show, so absurd and serene.

The tide rolls in, hoping to steal the scene,
As the palm trees sway with a rhythm unseen.
An octopus juggles, what a sight to behold,
In this paradise where laughter unfolds.

Echoes of the Island Heart

Laughter hangs in the warm ocean breeze,
While crabs have a party, just do as they please.
The toucans squawk jokes, and everyone chuckles,
In this land of bananas, coconuts, and buckles.

A parrot's a poet, reciting with style,
Making waves with his words, always worth a while.
The palm fronds shimmy, enjoying the jest,
As the sun sets laughing, it's simply the best.

With a splash and a dash, the fish keep it bright,
Making puns as they leap, what a glorious sight!
The sea turtles nod, like old pals who know,
That this island living never gets slow.

Echoes of giggles float over the bay,
As the stars take the stage at the end of the day.
Oh, what a joy, in this vibrant domain,
Where fun is the currency, and smiles reign.

Moonlit Shadows on Sand

Moonlight tickles the soft golden shore,
Where shadows play tag, and crabs start to roar.
A sandcastle kingdom is built with great glee,
While the tide giggles softly, 'Come play with me!'

Starfish spin tales of their watery dreams,
While seagulls bellyache about lost fish schemes.
"Why don't oysters donate to charity?" they croon,
"Because they are shellfish!"—cackles the moon.

The beach bums dance with an unshakable sway,
As the night pulls them closer, with mischief at play.
The tide brings in secrets from far-off lands,
While the shadows play pranks with the night's gentle hands.

In the distance, a mermaid is laughing out loud,
At the seaweed dancers, all tangled and proud.
As the stars jive above in a cosmic delight,
This moonlit fiesta carries on through the night.

Embrace of the Ocean's Caress

The ocean waves tickle my toes with a laugh,
As fish in tuxedos form a goofy staff.
Seashells gossip about tidepool affairs,
While crabby comedians pull funny old snares.

The sun sets low, and the sky bursts with color,
While starfish take selfies, all laughing and holler.
A dolphin named Joe tells a knock-knock joke,
As the moon joins the fun with a wink and a poke.

Sandcastles wobble, they're ready to fall,
As kids try to catch them—oh, what a ball!
The whispers of waves share secrets they'll keep,
In the embrace of the ocean, laughter runs deep.

With each rolling wave, there's a new tale to claim,
Of turtles who surf and crabs with no shame.
In this jolly paradise, life's a big play,
Where the ocean's bright giggles never fade away.

Quietude in the Jungle's Heart

In the jungle, a sloth took a seat,
He snoozed on a vine, not much of a feat.
A toucan named Fred, with colors so bright,
Sang off-key songs, bringing laughs to the night.

Monkeys in pajamas played tag with a goat,
While parrots debated who'd win the next vote.
The breeze whispered secrets, so silly and sweet,
As laughter erupted, no one faced defeat.

A snake wearing glasses sat reading a book,
While frogs in tuxedos made quite the cook.
They stirred up a stew of jokes and delight,
And danced on the leaves under soft silver light.

So in the heart of the jungle so wide,
Laughter and joy took a fun-filled ride.
From start to the finish, it didn't take long,
For nature joined in with their whimsical song.

Symphony of Treetops and Tides

A turtle on top of a palm tree did sway,
With his sunglasses on, he had come out to play.
A crab in a bowtie danced on the sand,
While the fish in the ocean played maracas so grand.

Bamboo flutes played by a monkey named Lou,
Sent ripples of giggles, a symphonic view.
The raccoons conducted with tails held up high,
As the parrots chirped tunes that fell from the sky.

Coconuts bounced to the beat of the drums,
While iguanas swayed, shaking off all their crumbs.
A fishy opera echoed far and wide,
As nature performed in a vibrant tide.

When the concert concluded, a standing ovation,
From creatures and critters, a joyful sensation.
Amidst all the music, a wise old toucan,
Said laughter is life, and it's better with jam!

Laughter in the Mango Grove

In the grove of the mangoes, a party took flight,
With elephants dancing, oh what a sight!
A squirrel in a tutu twirled under trees,
While bees held a bash with sweet honeyed breeze.

Cousins the monkeys played pranks on the bees,
Who buzzed in a flurry, "Now that's just not nice!"
They dipped into nectar, a sugary thrill,
And joined in the mischief with giggles and shrill.

A parrot at karaoke tried singing his tunes,
But each note he hit sent the others to swoon.
Coconuts giggled as they rolled on the ground,
In the laughter-filled grove, pure joy could be found.

So raise up your glasses of mango and cheer,
To friendships and laughter, let's draw even near.
In the grove where the silly and sweet come alive,
Each moment and memory helps laughter thrive.

Flickering Fireflies at Dusk

As the sun dipped low, fireflies came out,
With a glow like the stars, they danced all about.
A cricket named Carl led a shoelace parade,
And the frogs joined in, quite a spectacle made.

With tiny top hats and sparkly wings,
They hopped around joyously, laughing at things.
A ladybug leapt, wearing glasses so wide,
As a beetle rolled by on a miniature ride.

The moon peeked down, with a curious grin,
At the ruckus below, he could hardly begin.
An owl hooted softly, "Hey, what's all this noise?"
But the creatures just giggled, enjoying their joys.

So as dusk wrapped around in its shimmering veil,
Fireflies painted laughter like stars in the pale.
In a world full of wonder, with friends by our side,
Each evening laughs madly, a magical ride.

Essence of the Coconut Breeze

Coconuts crash on my head, oh dear,
A spa treatment I didn't want here!
Sipping from shells like a pirate's delight,
I thought I was clever; I lost that fight.

Swaying palms in a dance so wild,
Even the monkeys are laughing, beguiled.
Chasing the breeze, I trip on my toes,
The laughter of nature just grows and grows.

Seagulls swoop down for a fruity snack,
No respect, those birds, they just want to attack!
My picnic is chaos, is that a fish?
My sandwich is now part of their wish.

Yet here I'll stay, in this goofy place,
With sand in my sandals and joy on my face.
A vacation for laughs, who needs to unwind?
Life's better in giggles, leave worries behind.

Lullaby of the Surging Tides

The waves are a symphony, splashing in fun,
Sometimes they miss me; whoops, there goes my bun!
The ocean serenades with a gurgly sound,
While crabs think they're kings, strutting all around.

Surfboards pile high like a jumbled mess,
I try to get on, but I can't make progress.
A wipeout awaits, and I scream with glee,
Flopping like fish, oh look, that's just me!

Seashells whisper tales of mishaps galore,
I found one that's pretty, then slipped on the shore.
Riding the waves, oh, what a sight,
As I belly flop in the glow of moonlight.

The lullaby continues, I dance with the tide,
With laughter so loud, I can't even hide.
I'm a mermaid in training with much to learn,
But in this comedy, my heart takes its turn.

Serenade of the Exotic Night

The moon is a spotlight on a stage of delight,
Bugs sing their songs, creating a fright.
Fireflies twinkle like stars that are near,
But what's that buzzing? I think it's a beer!

Tropical fruits, all ripe and divine,
I tried to eat one, now I'm tangled in vine.
A lizard pops out, gives me a wink,
We both share a laugh as I spill my drink.

The night air is thick, full of giggling charm,
I tread softly, but wait, what's that alarm?
A parrot squawks loudly, "You dance like a fish!"
I blush in the dark, it's a friendly burn wish.

Yet here in this party, where stories unite,
With chatter and laughter, everything feels right.
I'll dance with the critters, drink a toast to my plight,
In this serenade, I'll lose sleep tonight!

Canvas of the Setting Sun

The sun dips low like a painter's swift brush,
Colors explode in a delightful rush.
I try to capture this beauty so grand,
But the paint spills over, now it's on my hand.

Sandy toes wiggle, feeling the heat,
As I trip over seashells, oh what a feat!
The sunset like cotton candy in the sky,
And I'm just a kid who forgot how to fly.

Barbecues sizzling with a smell so divine,
I throw on a burger, then lose track of time.
Seagulls plot heists on my plate of delight,
I wave like a maniac—shoo them outright!

Yet this canvas is lively, full of pure cheer,
With friends by my side, I hold them all dear.
As colors fade softly, my laughter ignites,
Under this sky, fun becomes the highlights.

A Chorus of Singing Crickets

At sunset's brush, they take the stage,
Crickets croon, in nature's rage.
Grasshoppers join, a hopping spree,
With every note, it's pure comedy.

A frog hops in, to steal the show,
Wearing a hat, quite the faux pas, though!
With every chirp, the rhythm kicks,
As fireflies dance, our laughter sticks.

A serenade of funny faces,
Laughter echoes in these wild places.
Each jump is met with a chuckle and cheer,
As nighttime falls, we hold our beer.

Together they sing, true harmony,
Nature's jest shows pure irony.
A gathering of tunes, a silly affair,
In this cricket concert, all hearts lay bare.

Blossoms Beneath a Gilded Horizon

Petals sway in a gentle breeze,
Bees in bow ties aim to please.
Flowers giggle at their bumbling cheer,
While butterflies stumble, oh dear, oh dear!

Sunshine tickles the maids of bloom,
As daisies plot their pranking doom.
With a flip and a spin, they hold their ground,
In this silly garden, joy's always found.

The roses chat about scandalous scents,
While vining with laughter, such merriment.
A tulip trips, falls onto the grass,
Creating laughter, oh how we amass!

Beneath the glow, of a brightening morn,
Nature's laughter, always reborn.
With petals that giggle, and bees that tease,
In this magical realm, we find our ease.

Reflections on the Coral Shore

Waves flip coins upon the sand,
Crabs wearing shades, look oh so grand.
Seagulls squawk jokes, soaring high,
As fish below laugh, saying 'Oh my!'

A starfish winks with a cheeky grin,
While clownfish swim in a colorful spin.
Sandcastles tumble in playful strife,
As children giggle, embracing life.

The tide rolls in, a slippery prank,
Splashing all, their laughter hangs plank.
Each wave's a joke that leaves us reeling,
Making this beach, the best place for feeling.

As sunset paints all in golden hue,
We dance in the waves, just us few.
Together we share these moments for sure,
Reflections of laughter, life's sweetest allure.

Rhythm of the Rainforest

In the jungle's heart, where the fun is loud,
Monkeys swing about, so proud, so proud.
Parrots chatter secrets, quite the chatterbox,
While sloths just wink, taking stock.

Each raindrop falls like laughter's spree,
Hitting leaves, creating a symphony.
Geckos dance on branches, sleek and sly,
While frogs croak jokes, oh my, oh my!

The vines hang low, with giggling grace,
As squirrels play tag in this wild space.
Nature's jesters perform with flair,
In this rainforest, we breathe the air.

With every rustle and every cheer,
The rhythm flows, bringing us near.
In the jungle's laughter, we find our way,
Under this canopy, we seize the day!

Lighthouses Guarding Moonlit Dreams

Lighthouses wink with bright delight,
Keeping watch all through the night.
Seagulls giggle, swirling around,
Their antics bright, a comic sound.

Moonbeams dance on waves below,
Whispers of fish in a silvery show.
I swear one flipped with a cheeky grin,
It's a party where they all spin!

A sailor trips on a jellyfish,
Cursing the sea for the splashy swish.
Turtles chuckle, hiding in shells,
Watching his splash like a clown's jells!

The lighthouse beams a hearty laugh,
As the ocean waves do their silly craft.
With dreams afloat, let joy ignite,
What a ridiculous moonlit night!

A Tapestry of Island Hues

Colors collide in a joyful spree,
Coconuts joke, 'Let's hang on a tree!'
Palm fronds wave with such pride,
While crabs scuttle, seeking to hide.

The sun bursts forth like a clown at play,
Turning the ocean to glittery spray.
Shells wear smiles, oh what a sight,
A rainbow parade in the morning light!

Artists painting with laughter and sun,
Fish in bow ties jumping for fun.
The sky blushes as if it might,
Join the island in this silly flight!

Under the treetops, monkeys groove,
Swinging along to the playful move.
In a patchwork of colors, all join the cheer,
A tapestry woven with joy sincere!

Dreams Adrift on a Gentle Sea

Dreams set sail on a wave so bold,
A boat of giggles, with stories told.
Fish in top hats swim by with style,
While sailors burst into laughter, all the while.

Clouds float by, resembling ice cream,
Casting shadows on waves like a whimsical dream.
Riding the tide, they wear goofy grins,
Bobbing along where the fun begins!

Starfish play cards on the sandy floor,
Shells join in, oh what a score!
The sea sings songs of playful cheer,
While quirky dolphins dance without fear.

A gentle breeze tickles the night,
With dreams that prance in pure delight.
On a raft of hope, we float with glee,
Finding joys adrift on this quirky sea!

Rhythm of Parrots at Daybreak

At daybreak's call, a raucous choir,
Parrots squawk with most playful fire.
They dance on branches, colors ablaze,
Singing tunes that amaze in all ways!

With beaks like paintbrushes, they do sway,
Creating beats to welcome the day.
The sun peeks through with a beaming grin,
While monkeys clap, joining in!

Mangoes fall, they weather the thrill,
As parrots plot more, it's their skill.
They nibble and giggle, causing a scene,
Life in the canopy, vibrant and keen!

Echoes of laughter ripple the air,
Like merry confetti floating everywhere.
In this wild serenade, let joy enlight,
With the rhythm of parrots, morning feels right!

The Allure of Coral Shores

The sands are hot, my toes turn red,
I chased a crab, tripped, and fled.
The seagulls squawk, they steal my fries,
I laugh as they plot their next surprise.

With sunburned noses and silly hats,
We giggle at strangers, just like cats.
A beach ball flies, it hits a chap,
He stumbles, oh what a silly flap!

Children build castles, but they all fall,
One kid yells out, "Hey, look at my wall!"
Their masterpiece is a mound of mud,
And all around there's laughter and thud.

As sunset gleams with shades of gold,
We toast with drinks that are very bold.
A slip, a splash, a tumble, a cheer,
Who knew the shore could be so near?

Chasing Sunsets in Color Splashes

With brushes dipped in sunset hues,
We paint the sky, no time to snooze.
A friend spills red into the blue,
And now it's purple - what's a girl to do?

Our art's a mess, but oh, the fun!
A chase for colors, oh, we run.
We step in puddles, where paint does flow,
Then slip and slide—it's quite the show!

The sun sets low, we wave it goodbye,
But wait! Who painted that smudge in the sky?
We giggle and point, like detectives on a case,
Trying to solve this colorful space.

As stars come out, we still make a fuss,
With giggles and stories riding the bus.
Each hue a memory, oh what a blast,
Chasing sunsets, we wish they could last!

Fragments of Paradise in the Air

A parrot squawks with quite the flair,
It stole my hat—did it just dare?
I chased it round, my flip-flops flew,
While locals laughed, I just turned blue.

The breeze is warm, it fluffs my hair,
I spot a dolphin, with elegant flair.
It leaps and spins—oh, what a show!
But all I can think is, "Is that my toe?"

Mango drinks spill, oh what a sight,
We slurp and giggle late into the night.
A dance competition breaks out in the sand,
My moves are wild—who needs a plan?

Fireflies twinkle, the sky brings cheer,
We bond over laughter, the best souvenir.
As stars twirl above, we feel so air,
Fragments of paradise floating in the air.

The Dance of Firelight and Stars

The bonfire blazes, and sparks take flight,
We roast marshmallows, oh what a sight!
A stick catches fire—yikes, oh dear!
That's not how you toast! Let's give a cheer!

We dance around, with spirits so bright,
Stumbling on toes in the warm twilight.
A crab joins in, it claps its claws,
A night of laughter, and endless applause.

With twinkling stars, we tell ghostly tales,
But the real fright? The smell of our gales.
Each core we bite brings bursts of delight,
While fireflies join, what a fun sight.

So here we are, with hearts all aglow,
Wiggles and giggles in the sand below.
As firelight dances and the stars align,
We laugh 'til our cheeks are rosy and fine.

Shadows Lengthen at Silver Hour

As daylight dips, the shadows creep,
The crabs on the shore seem half asleep.
A seagull squawks a nonsense tune,
While dolphins dance beneath the moon.

Beach umbrellas sway with flair,
One takes off! Boy, what a scare!
Flip-flops fly as people run,
Chasing shade, it's all in fun.

The sandcastles watch with pride,
As waves come in, their walls collide.
Kids yell out, "Look! There's a mermaid!"
Turns out it's just Dad, unafraid!

With laughter shared, we take a seat,
While crabs parade on wobbly feet.
As the sun dips low, it's clear as day,
Life's just a giggle in every way.

Kiss of Salt and Sunshine

Tropical breezes twist and twirl,
While beach balls bounce and seashells swirl.
Kids spill drinks, it's quite the sight,
Their giggles echo, pure delight.

The sandman builds with flair and grace,
A castle that's more of a dirt vase.
He points with pride, "Look at my throne!"
A wave comes in and it's overthrown!

The surfboards wobble, the surfers glide,
One takes a tumble, slips with pride.
A splash of salt, a face full of foam,
He stands up laughing, "Guess I'm home!"

With tuna sandwiches stuck to our toes,
We giggle as everyone knows,
That fun in the sun's the best of all,
Especially when your friends take a fall!

Melodies of the Hibiscus

In the garden where colors collide,
Hibiscus blooms with a grin wide.
The butterflies dance, it's quite a show,
Who knew flowers had such flow?

A parrot nearby begins to jest,
"I'm a great singer, just ask the nest!"
He screeches loudly, a comical tune,
Singing songs to the light of the moon!

The gardener trips, his hat takes flight,
It lands on a tulip! Oh, what a sight!
With dirt on his nose and a chuckle in tow,
He mumbles to blooms, "Can't steal the show!"

Amidst the laughter and vibrant hues,
Each petal whispers, "You can't lose!"
For in this place of joyous bliss,
Nature's humor is hard to miss!

Twilight's Embrace on Soft Sands

As twilight settles on soft gold sands,
The beachcombers stroll, collecting strands.
One found a shell that looks like a shoe,
He tries it on, and we all just coo.

The tides bring tales of pirates bold,
With toys galore, their secrets unfold.
In the distance, a grouchy crab yells,
"Hey, cut it out! This is no hotel!"

The bonfire crackles with giggles and cheers,
While marshmallows fly, igniting our fears.
A sticky mishap, oh what a mess,
"Who thought s'mores could lead to distress?"

As the stars twinkle, we share a grin,
Each moment a treasure, where laughter begins.
In this twilight embrace, we finally see,
Life's funny moments are best shared with glee!

Castaway Hearts on Sandy Beaches

We built a castle, oh so grand,
With seashell towers made by hand.
But then the tide came rolling in,
And turned our dream to sandy sin.

A crab became our trusty steed,
With tiny claws, it took the lead.
We raced the waves, we laughed out loud,
As gulls around us formed a crowd.

An empty coconut, our only chair,
We lounged like kings without a care.
Until a wave came with a crash,
And left us drenched—oh what a splash!

A treasure map, we found one day,
But it led us right to yesterday.
The X was marked on someone's toe,
We never know, we just say "whoa!"

Whirlwind of Colors in Paradise

There's a toucan wearing shades so bright,
Dancing on trees from day till night.
His beak that's rainbowed, such a sight,
He steals the show—oh, what a fright!

The iguanas join the funky beat,
Doing the cha-cha with happy feet.
But they only jiggle and wiggle slow,
Their style, a marvel—don't you know?

A parrot squawks, "It's fiesta time!"
As he hurls coconuts with a rhyme.
We dodged and weaved, then burst with glee,
In this circus of color and tropical spree!

Caught in a whirlwind of vibrant cheer,
With each silly twirl, we draw up near.
The sunset paints the sky so grand,
While giggles dance across the sand.

The Heartbeat of Mango Trees

Mangoes drop like whispers from the sky,
While nearby monkeys leap and fly.
We gather fruit for a juice-filled spree,
Oh, how we giggle, just wait and see!

A blender here is buzzing loud,
As monkeys throw a mango crowd.
We dance around each sticky spill,
Laughing as we chase our thrill.

Bees join in our humming song,
While we pick fruit the whole day long.
With laughter and juice, we start to sway,
In a fruity madness that won't decay.

The trees keep swaying, they hold the beat,
The vibrant life in every sweet treat.
We'll toast to nature, never shy,
Here amidst the mango sky!

Gentle Rain on a Shimmering Sea

Pitter-patter on our heads it falls,
While we dance barefoot to nature's calls.
Our beach ball floats away with glee,
As raindrops play a symphony!

We wear our shells as fun-filled hats,
And spin like tops along with splats.
The dolphins laugh, they think it's grand,
This water game across the sand.

Umbrellas fly like kites in fright,
While we splash joy in this delight.
The rainbow arcs come out to shine,
In this wacky weather, we sip our brine.

So come and join this silly spree,
Where showers lead to jubilee.
In every drop, we find our cheer,
As life spins round in this atmosphere!

Vibrance of the Twilight Palette

A parrot dances with flair,
Gossiping with a silly stare.
The sun dips low, a bright orange glow,
While iguanas roll like they're on a show.

Coconuts bounce, they're feeling spry,
As monkeys swing and laugh, oh my!
Palm trees sway, they don't seem to care,
While crabs do the cha-cha, oh what a pair!

The beach ball flies with joyful cheer,
Chasing sandcastles where dreams appear.
A toucan drops its snack with a plop,
And the laughter echoes, it just won't stop!

So let the colors play their game,
In this playlist of sunshine, oh what a name!
Where every sunset brings a giggle bright,
Painting the twilight with joy and delight.

Glimpse of Serenity Beyond Waves

Waves tickle toes as they rush and play,
Dolphins giggle, what a funny ballet!
Fish in shades of neon like to prance,
While sea turtles join in the quirky dance.

Flip-flops squeak, a comic soundtrack,
As beachcombers wander, never look back.
A seagull swoops for snacks on a plate,
While kids build towers, some leaning on fate.

Sandmen topple with a gentle nudge,
While sunscreen warriors refuse to budge.
A crab craves freedom, to scuttle and roam,
But ends up trapped in a beach ball's dome.

Each sunset ripples with gleeful tunes,
As starfish join in the rave of the moons.
Laughing together, the sea's jovial vibe,
Bringing mirth and joy to our happy tribe.

Horizon of Dreams and Delights

Kites fly high, painting the air,
While sunbathers bask without a care.
Laughter erupts from a picnic spread,
Where ants plot schemes to raid the bread.

Surfboards tumble like playful ducks,
As surfers attempt their best tricks and plucks.
A juice stall spills a fruity surprise,
Leaving sticky hands and blissful sighs.

Chasing sunsets, the sky's a grand show,
With flamingos striking a pose, oh so slow.
The horizon, a palette of giggles and cheer,
Filling our hearts, bringing friends near.

Wobbly tables filled with bright delights,
As mosquitoes throw their own crazy flights.
But beneath this scuffle and merry spree,
Lies the joy of laughter, wild and free.

A Tapestry of Colorful Tropics

Bright blooms giggle in the morning sun,
As bees wear tiny hats, they're so much fun.
The breeze tickles the leaves with a grin,
While lizards engage in a game of spin.

Parrots gossip about the best shade,
Admiring the antics the monkeys have made.
Flowers sway to the tunes all around,
Creating a symphony of joy unbound.

Tropical fruits make a juggling scene,
As folks run in circles, what a routine!
Melons and papayas bounce with delight,
While laughter fills the air, oh what a sight!

Each color a story, each laugh a song,
In this vibrant realm, where we all belong.
So come join the fun, bring your best smile,
In this tapestry of wonder, stay for a while.

Enchantment of the Gentle Surf

Waves jump high, they splash with glee,
Crabs doing the cha-cha by the sea.
Children squeal as they run and dash,
A seagull snickers, steals a snack with a flash.

Sunblock's on, but it's in my eye,
Now I'm blinking like a surprised guy.
Sand sticking everywhere, oh what a mess,
I look like a beach-themed game of chess.

Surfboards tangled, laughter fills the air,
But where's my flip-flop? I might despair!
Sun hats flying, catching a breeze,
Chasing them down? Oh please, not with ease.

Ice cream melting, drips on my toes,
The seagulls cackle, what a show they pose.
Lively moments, under the sun's reign,
Creating memories, like a wild, fun train.

Whispers in the Palm Leaves

Palms sway gently with a cheeky grin,
Talking secrets of the days that have been.
Lizards flipping, a show on the wall,
Coconut's rolling, oh! Here comes the fall.

Last night's party still on my mind,
Did I really dance with a fruit? So unrefined!
Pineapples chuckle, they know the score,
Mangoes gossip behind the fruit store.

Sunshine giggles as it creeps through,
Tickling noses, and melting the dew.
Every breeze whispers a tale of fun,
Like mischief brewed by a mischievous sun.

Stop and listen to the rustling cheer,
Palm leaves gossiping, they make it clear.
In this wild chatter, laughter takes flight,
Who knew nature had such a comical bite?

Dancing Shadows of Sunset

As the sun bows down, shadows extend,
I trip on my flip-flops, this fun won't end.
Sugar-sand dreams make me feel alive,
In this ballet of dusk, we all strive.

Firefly disco in the fading light,
Tiny dancers swirling, oh what a sight!
My shadow does the worm, it's the latest craze,
Is that my dance move? Or just a maze?

Tanning on towels, we strike a pose,
But a breeze sends my hat flying, oh no!
Laughter erupts as it lands on a stranger,
Who looks at me like I'm voice of danger.

In the twilight glow, waves softly sigh,
Making memories as stars start to fly.
Every chuckle and giggle, we'll hold so dear,
Dancing shadows of sunset, let's give a cheer!

Lullabies from the Ocean Breeze

The ocean hums a soft lullaby,
But who knew jellyfish are shy?
They float like artists, painting with lights,
While crabs throw raves on the sandy nights.

Gentle whispers in the salty air,
Seagulls serenade, they're quite the pair.
Shells chime in, each a unique sound,
As sea stars groove, they're so unwound.

Waves crash softly, but then they trip,
Hiccuping surf, oh what a slip!
Every splash sounds like a cheeky joke,
As dolphins giggle, they give a poke.

In this symphony of nightfall's charm,
Palms sway gently, with serene calm.
With each lullaby from the ocean's delight,
We drift into dreams, where all feels right.

Horizon's Edge at Day's End

The sun dips low, a big red ball,
Palm trees sway, they seem to call.
A pelican snorts, a crab gives a cheer,
"Come join the fun, we're all gathered here!"

Laughter erupts from the beach down below,
As tourists practice their limbo show.
A flip-flop flies, hits a guy on the leg,
He trips on a towel, oh what a peg!

The seagulls squawk in a playful dance,
One steals a sandwich, not leaving to chance.
As night descends, the glowworms shine bright,
Even the starfish are laughing tonight!

So raise your drinks, let's toast to the scene,
Where flip-flops are kings and the sun's always keen.
Tomorrow we'll sunbathe, but for now, let's play,
Life's a fun beach trip, come join the hooray!

Mysteries of the Moonlit Cove

In moonlit cove where shadows creep,
An octopus dances from his deep sleep.
He wears a top hat, quite dapper you see,
And invites us to join in his great jamboree!

A lobster tells jokes, he's quite the stand-up,
His claw waves about, and the fish all erupt.
"Why did the shrimp share his treasure at sea?"
"Because he was krilled with kindness!" Oh wee!

The waves giggle too, they lap at the shore,
While dolphins do flips, calling, "Give us more!"
The stars wink above, as if they conspire,
With tides and giggles, like a fun choir.

So if you get lost in the night's playful thrills,
Just follow the laughter and light from the hills.
In moonlit cove, all worries will flee,
For every night's hidden is pure jubilee!

Canvas of Shadows at Dusk

As daylight dims, the colors blend,
The horizon's a masterpiece, on that we depend.
A turtle winks, with paint on his shell,
"I'm an artist, you know?" He paints quite well!

The crickets chirp, launching a band,
Their legs strumming tunes in the soft, warm sand.
A parrot sings out but forgets half the words,
He fumbles and flutters, just humming like birds!

The beachballs bounce, all rolling around,
A kid kicks one hard, it sails with a sound.
Watch out for the palm trees, they're not quite your friend,

One sways to knock out a drink at the end!

So dance in the shadows, laugh at the night,
With every stumble and slip, it feels just right.
The canvas of dusk is a vivid delight,
With a squeeze of lime, we toast till it's light!

Secrets Told by Coconuts

A coconut sways from a high palm tree,
Whispering secrets, quite nuttily.
"Did you hear about Gary, the gull with a dream?"
"He wants to fly high, or so he does scream!"

The iguanas chuckle, wearing cool shades,
As they lounge on branches, in sun-kissed parades.
A pineapple jokes it can dance like a star,
But only when no one's watching too far!

The tides roll in with a splash and a clap,
Bringing surfboards and laughter, the ultimate map.
Coconuts giggle, their husks shaking tight,
Each secret they share adds to pure delight.

So gather round friends, the tales are a blast,
Where summer's a season that's meant to last.
In the shade of the palms, with laughter on cue,
We'll soak up the sun, just me and you!

Echoes of Joy from the Shoreline

Waves dance to a quirky beat,
Seagulls join in, they think it's neat.
Sunburned tourists pull a face,
While sand sticks in every place.

Flip-flops fly, oh what a sight,
Caught a crab, he's rolled in fright!
Laughter bubbles in the air,
As beach balls bounce without a care.

Ice cream drips, melts on my toes,
Caught by surprise, my laughter grows.
Coconuts fall with a loud thud,
While I just sit here—what a dud!

Surfboards wobble, a comical ride,
As everyone tries to hide their pride.
Yet joy echoes from the shore,
In silly antics, who could ask for more?

The Enchantment of Distant Drums

A rhythmic beat from far away,
Calls us to dance, oh what a play!
Hips sway left, then right, oh dear,
"Who's leading?" we all loudly cheer.

Drumsticks fly with joyful grace,
As someone trips, oh what a face!
Feathers jiggle, hats unhook,
While conga lines begin to look.

A twist, a turn, a spin so grand,
In this madness, all hand in hand.
Wild laughter fills the tropical air,
As we dance like we just don't care.

Though two left feet may trip our fun,
Each giggle proves we've already won.
In a world where rhythm's supreme,
We find joy in every dream!

The Sweetness of Pineapple Skies

Beneath the glow of fruity sun,
Pineapples tumble, oh what fun!
Sipping juice while wearing shades,
We laugh at life's delicious trades.

Straws do bend, and drinks just spill,
Sticky hands give quite a thrill.
We juggle fruits in silly shows,
Orange peels flying, look at those!

A blender whirls with laughter loud,
As we create our fruity crowd.
Smoothies splash, bright colors soar,
In every sip, we find galore.

A parrot squawks as we toast high,
To pineapple dreams up in the sky.
With fruity flavors making cheer,
We raise our cups—let's drink, my dear!

Starlit Reveries on a Quiet Move

Stars twinkle down—a playful prank,
As we stumble, our plans go blank.
Night's embrace brings joyful sight,
But who took the path, left, or right?

Flashlight beams become our guide,
While crickets chirp, let's take a ride.
Sudden shadows play peek-a-boo,
"Oh look! There's one, wait, where'd it flew?"

With giggles shared in moonlit glow,
We wander softly, cheeks aglow.
The night is ours, with silly schemes,
As we drift off into our dreams.

Instead of sleep, we giggle loud,
Creating memories, feeling proud.
For every step brings joy anew,
Beneath the stars and all they do!

Dreams Woven in Hibiscus

In a garden where laughter blooms,
The flowers dance to silly tunes.
A bee gets lost, oh what a sight,
Wearing pollen like it's a crown tonight.

Sipping drinks with floating ice,
A parrot squawks, "You'll look nice!"
Bananas giggle on their tree,
While coconuts crack jokes, carefree.

Sunshine tickles the ocean's face,
Waves that wobble with happy grace.
A crab tells tales of grand old days,
As seagulls roll their eyes and sway.

So let's toast with a coconut shell,
Full of stories we can't quite tell.
In this bloom of giggles and cheer,
Life feels best when friends are near.

Twilight's Song of the Islands

As the sun dips low, the stars arise,
Fish wear glasses, oh what a surprise!
The moon grins wide, a shiny disk,
Pushing a tide with a playful whisk.

Laughter floats like sweet perfume,
Dance with the crabs, make some room!
A toucan sings a catchy beat,
While geckos join in with tiny feet.

On the beach, a party vibes,
Where palm trees sway as the night jives.
A turtle slips in a beach ball game,
As they all cheer, "Hold the fame!"

With each wave a giggle gleams,
Silvery bubbles burst with dreams.
Underneath the winking sky,
Silly moments pass us by.

Mirage of the Floating Isles

On floating paths of bright blue dreams,
Where every puddle bursts at the seams.
A fish with legs tries to jump and cheer,
While sun hats land on a waiter's ear.

Pineapples wear sunglasses, so neat,
As the breeze plays the fanciest beat.
Coconuts roll into a conga line,
Yelling, "Come join, have some fun, it's fine!"

Clouds take a nap with no fuss at all,
While raindrops dance, having a ball.
A monkey swings with an ice cream cone,
Laughing so hard, it feels like home.

Under smiles of the sunlit sky,
Island fun makes worries shy.
In this mirage where dreams abound,
Every silly giggle is profound.

Kaleidoscope of Tropical Hues

In a prism of colors bright and bold,
A rainbow fish tells tales, retold.
With polka-dot patterns and fancy flares,
They swim with a snap, giggles in pairs.

Papaya plays a vibrant tune,
While a starfruit smiles at the moon.
Mangoes stumble, juggling with zest,
In this charming fruit dance, they are the best.

Lime and lemon have a laugh together,
Squeezing joy in sunny weather.
A thunderstorm with jester hats,
Makes puddles echo with cheerful chats.

Colors swirl in a playful way,
As laughter echoes every day.
In this kaleidoscope of cheer,
Fun blooms brightly, year after year.

www.ingramcontent.com/pod-product-compliance
Lightning Source LLC
Chambersburg PA
CBHW072135070526
44585CB00016B/1683